Journey to Soul

Discovering Your Authentic Life

Maggie Morris

The Journey To Soul: Discovering Your Authentic Life

Copyright © 2020. All rights reserved. No part of this publication may be reproduced, distributed, or transmitted to any form or by any means, including photocopying, recording, or other electronic, mechanical methods, without the prior written permission of the publisher.

As You Wish Publishing, LLC
Connect@asyouwishpublishing.com

www.asyouwishpublishing.com

ISBN-13: 978-1-951131-01-2

Library of Congress Control Number: 2020903233

Edited by Karen Oschmann

Printed in the United States of America.

Author Photo by Ami Holmes Photography

Nothing in this book or any affiliations with this book is a substitute for medical or psychological help. If you are needing help, please seek it.

Dedication

To my mother, Joan Edith Waddell, for without her support in life and in death, I may not have written this book.

To my beautiful children—my most precious treasures in this life. I truly believe you can find the enlightened life you were created to live.

To my partner, who believed in me enough to support this book effort and gave me the freedom to follow my passions.

To the tribe of people in my life, my mentors, guides, angels, as well as those who put up with my wounded self, and those who have encouraged me to heal and supported me as I continue to grow into my full potential as the authentic soul, Maggie.

Table of Contents

Foreword i
Introduction v
The Shelf 2
My Greatest Loss 8
Cardinal Visits 14
My Year Of Healing 20
Finding My Tribe 25
The Dinner, The Book 31
Death Doula 37
Letting The Wounds Speak 42
Walks With My Soul 45
Moments With Higher Self 49
The Gifts On The Porch 53
My First Speaking Engagement 59
The Changed Maggie—Without The Mask 72
The Vision, The Vibration, The Village 75
Soul Whispers From Maggie 79
About The Author 119

Foreword

My name is John Shearer. My purpose is helping people to connect with themselves and their spirituality by developing a mindful practice. Over the past eleven years, I have spent over nine thousand hours studying all aspects of mindfulness, especially in ancient cultures from around the world. That is why I now call myself a "Mindfulness Master." As a teacher, it is always my hope that the people who are touched by my ripple will then create a ripple of their own. That way, we can change the world, one person at a time!

One such person is Maggie Morris. I first met Maggie when she sent an email after my Facebook event, Mindfulness Day in 2015. In that email, she wrote, "Your book and this mindfulness journey have given me a new hope for the future in the next phase of my life. It feels like I have lived my whole life to get to this point. I want to encourage everyone I know and meet to embrace this mindfulness journey. What a dream it would be for young children to be taught this in our schools. I encourage my adult children to embrace it and live a mindful life one day at a time, one minute at a time."

Maggie went on to study mindfulness and now has every right to call herself a Mindfulness Master. Maggie has written this book and asked me to write a forward. I feel very honored to write this forward, for a book which she aptly named, *Journey To Soul*. Maggie fully realizes that a mindful practice is a spiritual practice that leads to awakening. You don't have to climb halfway up a mountain and sit cross-legged in a cave for five years to become enlightened. When you have both peace of mind and clarity of mind, no matter what is happening in your life, that's what I call awakening.

Maggie delivers in no uncertain terms! She writes about her suffering and takes us on a journey to give us a great understanding of our suffering. I believe we need suffering to help us appreciate life's joys and to be grateful for our time on this amazing planet. Maggie is the right person to write this kind of book because of her individual life experience. Her time as a hospice volunteer and death doula give us wonderful insights and a totally different perspective. I love how she uses language that is easy to understand and helps to give clarity to our experiences, especially the things that have often left us wondering.

Maggie delves into the world of mysteries and synchronicities that keeps us enthralled and entertained. We come to realize that there really are no coincidences. When we start living in the present moment with awareness, we notice the little things that often become the big things! Life doesn't pass us by anymore. Maggie helps us remove both our fears and our masks, making us more authentic and also a little bit more vulnerable. This, in turn, helps all our relationships and our connection to life and beyond. This is important because the world today seems to be focused on wanting more and getting more. Through her storytelling and affirmations, Maggie reminds us to *just be*!

Foreword

Maggie is set to create her ripple, and you will be more equipped to create your ripple. Together, we can make a difference in this crazy world. Be mindful—pause—connect!

John Shearer

John Shearer—Mindfulness Master and author of *Mindful Actions*, South Grafton, NSW Australia, 29th December 2019.

Introduction

I once thought I needed to find myself. Was I misplaced? Was I lost? No! I was *me*. But was I the me that I believed I was, or was I the me that my soul was created as? This is my journey to find my soul.

In my 60 years of living, life has taught me many things. Circumstance has taught me many things. People have taught me many things. Also, all a collection of potential books that you may or may not ever want to read.

But those things or beliefs, I took on as truths.

Are we who we truly are, or are we simply the accumulation of beliefs we chose to accept as who we are?

That is the deeper question I want to explore.

For each of us, those beliefs are as different as night and day, and as individual as our personalities and life experiences. That is why I can only write about my journey, my life, my experiences, but I invite you to allow my journey to ignite you to find your soul truth.

Very early on in my life I learned that I needed to fit in, find my place, be successful, find my purpose, seek love, and strive for perfection. As a little girl, this became my truth: I was not enough!

For many of you reading my book, this may be or may have been your truth as well. Let me be the beacon of light to you, *this is not your truth*, this is your belief—a belief that limits your true potential!

My soul truth is that *I am enough*. Your soul truth is that *you are enough*!

When we let go of the limiting beliefs that have kept us prisoners of our circumstances, we have the opportunity to step forth in the truth of who we truly are.

Yet in my experience, living, listening, and believing those limiting beliefs caused me to remain a victim of circumstance, suffering medical issues, anxiety, and depression, living an angry, unfulfilled, inauthentic life, and generally being unhappy. That is until I found the Soul Maggie.

The Soul Maggie is *enough*.

The Soul Maggie is *love*.

The Soul Maggie is *authentic*.

If you are a religious person, the Bible says that "we are created in the image of God." Theological educators will debate for a lifetime, the true meaning of that, but suffice it to say that being created in the image of God is enough.

To quote Rumi, "We are born of love. Love is our mother." We are all born into this world in the same way. We are all born to accept and give love.

Our soul is love

To give love

To receive love

Introduction

Love is *enough*!

Being authentic means coming from a real place within ourselves. From within myself, I am love; therefore, I can be authentic when I love myself.

Loving myself took effort on my part. I needed to let go of all those limiting beliefs that I had picked up over the years (and unfortunately still pick up). I needed to heal from the wounds those beliefs had caused over the years. Some wounds were quite deep, full of poison and scar tissue from continued wounding. I needed to let go of beliefs that no longer served me if I was going to live my authentic life. Those beliefs included the perfectionist, the need for acceptance, the need to fight to be right, and the need to constantly have "all my ducks in a row" and have life all figured out.

I needed to learn to live a life of nonjudgmental love for myself and others, which is a work in progress at the best of times.

I learned that my soul has the ability and desire to guide my life so that I am in the right place at the right time for the right things, and I can simply trust in that.

I learned that my soul would implant wisdom and direction for every circumstance that would ever come into my life, and I can simply trust in that.

Let me tell you a bit about that journey.

CHAPTER

The Shelf

I think it is less important to talk about how I was wounded and more important to talk about what I needed to overcome to connect with my soul on that journey to soul.

As humans, we all have wounds in this lifetime, some superficial, and some that cut deep into our being, fundamentally changing us. Let's just say, I was at the fundamentally-changed level.

In 2015, I experienced what I like to refer to as a "my shelf fell down moment." You know that shelf, the one where you put all the things you can't handle or just don't want to handle. Yes, you know the one I mean. Take a moment and look inward. What does your shelf look like? Is it loaded with stuff you have been carrying for way too long? Is it about to fall from the weight of it?

It is my prayer that you will find some insights in my journey to soul that will help you sort out that shelf before or after it falls down. I say before *or* after because healing and change can come in either circumstance. One is no less or better than the other, it just is.

I had been a hospice volunteer since 2014, and on this particular day, I was sitting in a seminar on caregiver fatigue and the importance of self-care. Although I had been a caregiver in one capacity or another for over 30 years, I had never heard of caregiver fatigue, and self-care

Chapter One | The Shelf

is when you jump in the shower for a few minutes, just hoping to be left alone and not fall as you rush to get out.

As I listened to the signs and symptoms of this caregiver fatigue, I quickly realized that it was not a good thing, and I was pretty much the poster child for it. I cautiously looked around to see if everyone was looking at me because I was sure there was a big flashing arrow over my head, letting everyone know I was the proud winner of this caregiver fatigue prize. Thankfully, that sign was only visible to my eyes, and everyone in the room was oblivious to the panic going on in my head. I sat quietly for the rest of the seminar, not even hearing much of it. The anxiety inside me was just too great!

The very next day, I made an appointment to see the therapist who was leading the seminar—surprisingly, within a few days.

Jane was a compassionate, understanding, and gentle therapist with a lot of expertise in her field of work. She listened to my story and, without any judgment, said she would happily guide me through change and most certainly felt I was correct in my self-diagnosis that I was indeed suffering from caregiver fatigue. Over the next few weeks, we had regular appointments and discussed how I had found myself with that shelf on the floor, although she said she had not heard it described quite that way before. After each session, she would send me on my way with some task to do to help me find my healing. She mentioned on more than one occasion that she was the guide, but I had to do the work of healing myself if I wanted change.

After one thought-provoking session, she suggested I look into meditation and mindfulness, as it could help me discover who I was and what inspired and made me happy. You see, in that session, she had asked me the most bizarre thing I had ever heard. Something that, to my knowledge, I had never been asked before that day. She simply asked what made me happy. I had no clue! Over 55 years old, and I had no clue what made me truly happy. I was heartbroken.

I went home to the faithful Google and was immediately connected with a mindfulness coach in Australia. If you need a mindfulness coach, I highly recommend you check him out at:

http://www.mindfulnesscoach.com.au and read his book *Mindful Actions*, where he authentically shares his personal journey.

Here I was in Canada, connected with a mindfulness coach in Australia, whose life story would impact my life in such a way that I would begin my quest to find my soul. How cool is that?

John Shearer took a chance on writing a book and being authentic about his life. His ripple expanded and touched my life. Wow! How cool is that?

Is it coincidence or a synchronized universal awakening at work? I believe that on that day, in that seminar, the Universe had begun to chart my course to find my soul and heal my life.

At another session, I mentioned to Jane that my head felt like a washing machine stuck on the spin cycle. Some

Chapter One | The Shelf

days I felt like I would just spin out of control. On that day, my homework was to go find out what "monkey mind" was. So off I went, back to my friend Google, to find out the meaning of monkey mind. Like Jane, I'm going to send you on a quest to find that too.

Just kidding, haha!

The term monkey mind refers to being unsettled, restless, or confused.

Here is the link to one article about it to get you started just in case you're not acquainted with my friend, Mr. Google: https://www.psychologytoday.com/ca/blog/the-empowerment-diary/201709/calming-the-monkey-mind.

In figuring out what monkey mind was, I also found out how to quiet that monkey. Over the years, my mind had been given a free pass to record my thoughts, real or unreal, and continually play that unsolicited recording back to me whenever it wanted.

It is my belief that listening to that unsolicited life recording causes much of the anxiety and depression in our world today.

My research had shown me that meditation and mindfulness were very helpful in quieting that monkey. Trust me, the monkey did not leave my head easily. It took much effort and practice on my part. And even still, there are times that little monkey tries to come home.

Please remember, your thoughts are neither right nor wrong, they just are! Read that again!

You can reprogram your brain through gratitude exercises and through the "I AM" mantras, as an example. Here is a little example to get you started, but I encourage you to find exercises and mantras that work for you.

https://www.drwaynedyer.com/blog/the-power-of-i-am/

So, that is my story on how I found meditation and mindfulness.

And yes, just in case you are wondering, I was able to put the shelf back up, but in doing so, I also decided that many things did not need to go back on it. Now, through mindful meditation, I gently and freely clear my shelf of life's unnecessary things that would weigh me down.

And the journey continues.

CHAPTER

My Greatest Loss

On September 11, 2017, at 4:20 a.m., my mom, Joan Edith Waddell, the first friend in my life, left this world for her next.

The journey to her death was both my greatest struggle and my greatest accomplishment. I'm not even sure I can write about it and give it the value or the recognition that the story deserves.

I must pause and ask God, my Creator, my angels, my spirit guides, my ancestors, and maybe even my sweet momma to help me write this chapter.

What happens in this chapter, in my opinion, is nothing short of a miracle, although I did not see it that way at the time.

My mom had lived with and suffered from congestive heart failure for many years, and had even been close to

Chapter Two | My Greatest Loss

death a few times, then she would rally back and live on. But not this time.

Early in the year of 2017, Mom was consistently becoming weaker and was requiring more care. She had fallen a few times, had been in and out of the hospital, and had begun her steady decline in health.

I was working full time. Healthcare was very limited in the services they offered, yet I knew Mom wanted to stay home. It was also important to me that she stay at home. My mom had lived with me for many years, loved me, and had been a supportive role in our lives. After my life catastrophe, which had left me a single parent with two young children, she had been a source of great love and support, so it was only natural that I would take care of her now when she needed care. However, that became increasingly difficult, as there were not enough support systems in place to help me, or at least that I was aware of at the time.

We decided that my sister and her husband, who were both retired, would stay at my home and help. They were a Godsend, and I don't think I would have survived without their help. Our home eventually became her hospice. With my training and work at hospice, I was able to find out how to access the help that we received. Trust me—even with my connection to hospice, it was not always an easy process to find services. Congestive heart failure (CHF) is not like many other terminal illnesses, as there is no known "death plan." That made accessibly to services sometimes more difficult. But we continued on.

Within a few months into the year, my sister and husband had completely moved into my home to help, as Mom could no longer be left alone.

By April of that year, I decided it was time to take a leave of absence from work, as I knew she was not going to get better this time. I could not be at work while my mom, the one who loved me first in life, was dying.

As she got worse, and eventually bedridden, she suffered from hallucinations and was in considerable pain. The PSW Home-Care workers came daily now, with nurses attending on a regular basis as well. She was dying, yet I still had difficulty getting her deemed palliative. Being put on the palliative list was important, as it enabled us to receive additional services, which we desperately needed.

Finally, on a particularly difficult day, the home care nurse came for her visit and witnessed Mom's (and my) distress. She became our angel as she sprang into action calling the doctor, hospice, the social worker, and insisting that the home hospice referral be made for my mom. Within days, the hospice home team was coming to us on a regular basis and continued to do so until her death.

At about ten weeks before her death, my mom was no longer able to eat or drink and had become increasingly uncomfortable. About eight weeks before her death, I talked with Mom about medical sedation and asked her if she would be more comfortable being sedated. At this point, and almost on a regular basis, she would ask to die or ask the nurses to end her life. She said for me to do whatever would take away her pain.

Chapter Two | My Greatest Loss

One day, at one of her more lucid moments, I remember her telling me that Jesus came to see her and told her that it wasn't her time yet, but he would be back soon for her. It brought her such peace. I joked with her that if he came by again to call me because I had a few things to ask him.

At about six weeks before her death, the medical team and I decided that sedation would be best for her. That day was bittersweet for me. I knew it was what was best for her because it would end her pain. But for me, it increased the pain, for I knew I would never again have another conversation with my mother. For as long as I live, I will never forget those sedation moments.

After the medication was injected, she was still having difficulty calming, so everyone left the room in case their activities were preventing her from calming. As I sat there holding her, tears streaming down my face, she started singing to me:

"I love you, you love me,

I'm as happy as I can be."

She continued singing to me as she slipped into sedation.

The next day when the nurse walked in, I burst into tears. She asked what was upsetting me, and through my tears, I said: "I will never hear her voice again." The nurse lovingly asked, "Do you want to bring her out of sedation?" Through my tears, I shook my head no. I knew the sedation was for her comfort, not mine. It was my final act of love for her! Much later, I would come to find out what her final act of love was to me, but that is another chapter.

For the next six weeks, almost daily, she would somewhat stir from sedation long enough to mouth the words, "I love you." The vision of that is forever etched in my mind.

Mom was sedated for six weeks before she passed from this life. Her journey became a case to study for the team because they could not understand why it was taking so long for her to die.

At 4:00 a.m., the morning she passed from this life on earth, I heard her call my name as clear as she did when I was a young child. I got out of bed immediately and went downstairs to where she was laying, with the overnight nurse sitting right with her. The nurse hurried me back to bed, assuring me that mom did not call out. Back to bed I went, only to hear her call to me again, just as clearly as the last time. I went back down again and sat on the steps a minute, watching her chest expand with each breath. Again the nurse said, "Go back to bed, honey, you need sleep." Within moments the nurse knocked on the door; my mom had passed away at 4:20 a.m. after calling my name twice.

Is it possible that Jesus had come back for her? Was she calling to tell me just as she had promised she would when he came back for her?

My greatest loss had suddenly become my greatest life accomplishment.

In the next chapter, I will tell you about the strange happenings during that sedation time.

CHAPTER

Cardinal Visits

This chapter may be the biggest stretch for some of you, I know it took a while for me to digest it and come to the realization that quite possibly I did *not* lose my mind.

About a month after my mom's death, a co-worker and I were having a conversation over lunch one day. She proceeded to say to me, "Did I ever tell you I hear from dead people?" Nope, I'm pretty sure she had not. I'm pretty sure that would have been something I would have easily remembered.

She proceeded to tell me that while my mom was in her medical sedation, she used to come and talk with her. Ya, right! That's what I was thinking as well. However, she went on to tell me things that she claimed my mom had told her about me, things she would have had no way of knowing. You see, I had only worked with her for a few months before taking that leave to care for my mom, she had never been to my home, never met anyone in my family, and certainly had never met my mother. So how did

Chapter Three | Cardinal Visits

she hear these things? Could it even be possible that my mom had visited her in spirit? Does that even happen?

Over the next weeks, she would share more and more with me about these occurrences. She told me that each time, just before my mom would come to her, a cardinal would come to her window and start calling out to her. Whether she was at work, at home, or in the car, the cardinal would appear, and then my mom would come to her to talk.

Trust me, I know exactly how bizarre this all sounds! All I know is, it happened!

My co-worker went on to tell me about things in my life that caused me a deep woundedness, things that, as she said, my mother wanted me to heal from. Many of these things were things that only my mother knew, even some that no other human knew. The most impacting day was the day she told me that my mom and dad came together to speak with her and wanted her to tell me that the anger I carried for my father regarding my parents' divorce was my mother's pain, not mine. I was stunned and breathless. You see, my father had passed away many years before, and I knew that I had never spoken to this co-worker about my father or that my parents were even divorced. I was beginning to think that quite possibly she had spoken with my mom, yet the whole thing was beyond comprehension. My brain could not wrap my head around it. So I just sat with it a while and never told another person. I digested it, letting it sink deep into my soul.

She even said that I was asking my children to do something that I would not do myself. The instant she said that a picture flashed in my mind of me standing on my front porch with my son on the day of my mom's memorial, telling him that he needed to forgive his father for wounds of the past. It was like a lightning bolt went through me, and I knew exactly what she was talking about.

I knew this was serious shit she was sharing, and in that instant, I knew it was true!

That night I went home, and in meditation, I metaphorically stuffed everything that I had been holding about my father into a black balloon and released it. In my mind's eye, I watched the balloon fly away out of sight. Never again did I feel the pain I had been holding about my father. I felt a freedom that I had not felt for years.

One thing that kept coming back to me was something I had watched my mother do for many months. On most occasions, when people would visit Mom, I would hear her asking them, "Will you take care of Margaret when I'm gone?" (She never did call me Maggie.) I would get embarrassed each time, as I knew they would feel obligated to say yes to her, yet I knew no one could ever replace her in my life, nor would they want to "take care of" her adult child. Nevertheless, she continued to ask.

I wondered, is it possible that she got tired of asking and without getting the response she wanted, she had just taken it upon herself to take care of me? Was that even a possibility?

I considered all options, pondered it over in my mind for months, all while trying to figure out if I was losing my mind or if my co-worker had, and now she was somehow pulling me into her crazy.

Chapter Three | Cardinal Visits

Part of the protocol as a hospice volunteer is that when you suffer a significant personal loss, you are required to suspend working with the dying for a time of personal healing. I had scheduled my meeting with the hospice therapist for my return to work there. In that meeting with him, I decided, rather impromptu and without much advance consideration, to just plain ask the question and get his opinion on these visits between my mom and my co-worker. Possibly, if I had lost my mind, I would rather hear it from someone I barely knew than someone close to my life. After all, if he did think I was crazy, I could just never see him again and never go back to hospice. Easy problem solved.

Thankfully, he did not think I was crazy! In fact, he shared some very good insights. He explained that as he understood it, at death or dying, the veil between life and death becomes thin or opens. He said he has heard of times when, before death, the dying can at times actually travel between both realms. Wow! That actually made sense to me. Hallelujah, maybe I was still in my right mind!

Many articles support this theory. I attach just one for you to look at.

https://www.dyingmatters.org/page/spiritual-aspects-death

I now found myself open to the possibility that we may have found the reason why it took my mom so long to die. She was busy doing soul work for me! Her final gift to me in her life on earth was to set the course for my healed life! How freaking amazing is that?

My co-worker took a chance and was authentic in sharing her experiences in talking with my dying mom. Her ripple had expanded and touched my life. Wow! That ripple keeps showing up, expanding, flowing, and changing lives.

CHAPTER

My Year Of Healing

On New Year's Eve, December 31, 2017, I declared to the Universe that 2018 was my year of healing!

Well, I tell you, the Universe heard and replied with, "Challenge accepted!"

What a year it would turn out to be!

I truly wish I had been better at writing or journaling—had I ever thought I would be writing this little book, I certainly would have worked at being better at it. Sorry folks reading this, you get the authentic editorial, not the corrected edited perfected version.

So many pivotal things happened, I feel it's important to pause again and ask for help in what to share with you.

Again I ask God, my Creator, my angels, my spirit guides, my ancestors, please flow through me, inspire and write this chapter to give it the justice it deserves.

One of the pivotal occurrences that comes to mind is a dream walk with one of my spirit guides. In a dream, my spirit guide woke me up and asked me to go for a walk through my neighborhood with her. I got up, very inquisitively, and started walking down my street with her,

Chapter Four | My Year Of Healing

still not sure if I was awake or asleep. Have you ever had a dream where you see yourself lying in bed, still sleeping, but you are outside your body? Well, that was this dream. So vividly real!

As we walked along, I felt completely safe. Absolutely comfortable in the strangeness of this dream.

She said, "I have some things to show you. I want to show you how to feel knowingness."

We continued along as she spoke to me about how sometimes we can just feel things and get a knowing in our spirit. Along the way, she stopped in front of three houses on that block.

At the first house, she stopped and told me that there was a great sadness there.

At another, she simply said to feel the need.

At the third house, she told me, "They need love."

It's important to point out here that these were houses in my neighborhood. Actual houses where I may have seen the people on the street, but certainly not houses where I knew of circumstances within their homes or had personal relationships with them. At least I had not yet.

We ended that walk and stood together on my front porch. For descriptive purposes, I tell you that my front porch is covered but not closed in. It has some pillars and a roof on top.

As we stood on that porch, others started coming, and without saying a word, they placed things in the beams and along the window ledges of that porch. They left their items and silently walked away. I ask her what they were leaving there. She just smiled and said, "Honey, just some things you will need later." When they were finished, she just hugged me, smiled, and told me to go back to bed and get some rest.

In a future chapter, we will talk more about what I think those gifts were.

When I awoke in the morning, that dream was as vividly real as if I had truly lived it. Maybe I had? I had, after all, already experienced a few strange occurrences.

Before long, the person in the first house stopped me while I was walking my dog, and proceeded to tell me that his mother had just been diagnosed with cancer and would not have long to live. I felt his sadness. So much so, that I felt it the day she died. I knew before he even stopped me again to tell me that she had died. How bizarre that felt to me! I did not tell a single soul.

Before too much longer, each time I walked my dog past the second house, I felt this overwhelming urge to knock on the door and ask how they were doing. I had met this couple a few times; they were new to the neighborhood. They had been friendly and chatted with my dog on a few occasions, but I didn't know them well enough just to walk up and knock on their door. Who does that? That would just be insane? The urge continued, but each time I just walked past. One day as I was walking the dog, the man was outside in the driveway. What he said next almost caused me to faint! He proceeded to tell me that he had to have emergency open-heart surgery, and while recovering, he would see me walking the dog and

Chapter Four | My Year Of Healing

wished he could say hello. As I was walking past feeling that urge to knock on the door, he was inside wishing the dog and I would come to visit him. How completely bizarre is that?

The third house gets even stranger!

I was preparing to take a course on therapeutic touch. For unknown reasons, the original course was canceled. Before long, the instructor called me to say she was doing the course for some people from the Alzheimer's Society and had one spot left if I would like it. I agreed.

I went to the course on the scheduled day, in the next town, about 20 minutes from home. I was surprised when a lady walked in whom I had known years ago at a previous job; she was a customer of mine. Imagine my greater surprise when I found out later in the afternoon that she lived in the third house the guide had stopped in front of on my dream walk. It was certainly a real "holy wackadoodle" moment!

The real shocker came later when the instructor was talking about the founders of the therapeutic touch, Dolores Krueger and Dora Kunz, and passed around their pictures only for me to see that Dora Kunz was the lady from my dream walk. As I looked at her picture, I was sure I saw her wink, and I heard, "Hi Maggie, do you remember me?" Holy wackadoodle yet again! There I was right back in the "I think I've lost my mind" moment. I think I was able to accept it a little easier this time because these strange occurrences were becoming part of my new normal.

I became instant friends with the lady in house three.

Had Spirit or the Universe made those connections to teach me about love, intuition, and the knowing, as well as about angels, guides, and how our path is orchestrated by something greater than we can fathom? I now believe it is possible! I have learned to have more faith in my knowing. I have learned to believe that quite possibly, there is much more going on in this universe than our brains or wisdom can comprehend. Some things just don't fit the box that we create with our minds.

I invite all who read this book to be open to the possibility that there is much more happening in our universal realm than we can fathom with our human intelligence, and much more out there than schools educate on, or religious scholars teach about.

It took almost two years for that dream to play out in my reality realm, and I'm not even sure it completely has to its fullest as yet. Time means nothing in the spirit realm. Time operates in the earth realm. Remember that.

After all, there are still those "gifts" the guides left on the porch. It is my belief that some of those gifts left are healing modalities I have learned, and others may be spiritual connections I have made and will continue to make in years to come. One may even be this book!

CHAPTER

Finding My Tribe

When your life is dramatically spiritually changed like mine was, or like yours may be, it is important to find like-minded people to share life with. People to learn from and grow with.

I trusted that since the Universe had brought me this far, there was a strong possibility that I could rely on that same source to make connections in my life.

I have made many connections—some long term connections, and some came quickly in and out of my life to teach me something about myself.

Random chance happenstances are the best. But then again, I ask, are they truly random, or is it the result of synchronization in the spirit realm? I tend to believe that few things in life are random.

It was during one of those random occurrences that someone asked me if I had ever heard of Lily Dale. I replied that the only Lily Dale I had ever heard of was a brand of chicken. We laughed, as she was referring to the spiritualist community in Lily Dale, New York. Someone had told her about this town that has mediums, a healing temple, and various other spiritual events. I told her I had not heard of it and never gave it another thought.

Within that same week, another random person asked me if I had ever heard of Lily Dale. What are the odds?

Chapter Five | Finding My Tribe

This spiritual community has been established since 1879, and I had never heard of it, and now within a week of each other, two people mention it to me. This time, I did say that I knew it was not a brand of chicken. Strangely, that person began to question me about whether or not I had been experiencing a spiritual awakening. She said there was an aura about me that she had not noticed in previous meetings. She advised me that she believed I was supposed to visit Lily Dale, and that there would be a message there for me. This time I did give it a second thought; in fact, I gave it a lot of thought.

A few weeks later, I did travel to Lily Dale, New York, with my (now) daughter-in-law. I was intrigued and interested in finding out more about this place and the supposed message I was to find there. The place didn't look like much as you went through the gate, a little worn, some places were unkept, some beautiful homes, like a little hidden community. Somewhat like walking back in time.

We parked the car, got out, and instantly I felt something. I felt dizzy. There was energy unlike anything I had felt before. I was nervous, yet excited. You see, in my Christian background, I had been taught that mediums were of the devil, so I was cautious. I had trusted that Spirit would show me if this place was evil. So I cautiously ventured on.

I'm not sure if my anxiety was obvious or not, but as we walked into the little museum, I was greeted by a sweet lady. She asked if I had visited before, and I told her no, it was my first visit. Like she already knew my thoughts (maybe she did), she informed me that, although there is a dark side in the spirit realms, Lily Dale is in the light of Spirit and does not practice in the darkness. It was as if she knew what my mind was already questioning. The whole place seemed very tranquil and spiritual. It was a beautiful experience.

I had looked all day for the message I was to receive.

At the end of the day, I met with a medium called Mary. She was a sweet lady. At the end of our chat, she told me that I reminded her of herself because only five years ago, she was like me, a volunteer with her local hospice who had happened upon her own spiritual awakening. She told me that I needed to find my tribe, meditate, and see where this journey would lead me. Those words resonated with my soul. Was that my message? No, I believe the experience was the message.

A day or so after I arrived home, I got an email from my new friend, Mary. She said she studied with a woman from my town and wanted my permission to connect us. She did, and I visited that woman, we had a long chat about what had happened thus far in my journey. We chatted for over four hours. The woman was an inspiration. She invited me to find a meditation group and suggested I start to meet like-minded people.

Shortly after that, I visited my friend Google again in search of local meditation groups. I thought maybe it was time to reach out to those like-minded people. I had been on this healing journey for a while, and maybe it was time to include others.

I went to the one group that the lady recommended; it was large and only met once a month. I felt I wanted more

Chapter Five | Finding My Tribe

than a once a month group, and the large crowd was a little overwhelming to me. I felt it was easy to get lost in the crowd.

I happened upon Spiritual Awareness Niagara, sent an email for information, and a friendly lady responded to my request with meeting times. I went to the group a few times before I could actually get out of the car and go in. This was so far out of my comfort zone and caused me great anxiety. Funny isn't it, I'm going to a meditation group, and it's causing me anxiety. Sometimes in life, my friends, you have to push through the hard bit to get to the good stuff. For me, the hard bit was just walking in the door.

Once inside, I found the group welcoming, friendly, inclusive, and extremely informative. It seemed that each week the topic being discussed was closely related to stuff I had been learning about by myself. I learned a lot from those people and have come to refer to them as my tribe.

I encourage you if you are seeking a tribe. Ask the Universe to be your guide. Find a tribe of like-minded people and continue on your quest.

The Universe will always continue to expand your tribe to greater depths than you can ever imagine. That tribe will grow outside the confines of your imagination. Let go of control and let the Universe steer your course! You will get the ride of your life, full of wonder and possibilities!

CHAPTER

The Dinner, The Book

My partner's boss invited us to a "random" fundraising dinner. You know why I quote the word random, right? Because nothing is ever random!

His boss gave no information about the fundraiser, just that the tickets were a gift, get dressed up, and be ready for a fun night out. So we went. It was a fun night, just as promised.

The event, as it turned out, was a fundraiser for mental health awareness and initiatives. It truly was a fun, informative evening.

As we were leaving, we walked past a table with some books on it and a sign that said: "Please take one." The book was called, *My Kid is Driving Me CRAZY* by Tamara Arnold. I grabbed the book and took it with me.

The next day we were packing for vacation—a reading vacation for me, and a golf vacation for my partner—so I grabbed the book off the table and threw it in my suitcase. It was a small book, looked like an easy read, with quite a catchy title. In my reality, I happened to have a kid that was driving me a little crazy.

Chapter Six | The Dinner, The Book

One rainy day, while sitting in the resort, I picked up that book. Before I knew it, I had read the whole book! It was powerful! That woman had somehow written a book about my life. It was raw and authentically real.

Minutes after I closed the book, my cell phone rang. I picked it up, looked at the display, my daughter was calling. I answered, sure that something must be wrong for her to be calling me while I was on vacation. Bizarre! There was a bad snowstorm back in Canada, and thinking I had only gone away for the weekend, she said she was concerned if I was safe or traveling on icy roads. Even more bizarre, because for many years, she had not seemed to care if I was alive, let alone been concerned about my being safe.

A coincidence, or was Spirit sending me a message yet again? You know what I believe about coincidence and random occurrences, so I chose to believe that Spirit was up to something.

The author of the book had included her information at the back of the book, so I looked her up and sent her a message. She responded instantly, which really shocked me.

Here is the message copy I sent her:

I'm sitting in Myrtle Beach and just finished reading your book that I picked up at the mental health fundraising event last week.

It was amazing, real, and timely.

I am a mother surviving now-adult children with mental health issues.

The long and short of it is that 2018 is my year of healing myself.

Your book was placed in my hands by the Universe as part of that journey.

I knew nothing about the event we went to and only received an invitation three days before, being told only that it was a great evening out.

Thank you for the courage it took to write such an honest book. And so true!

As I said to someone a few months ago, I have taken care of people for over half my life. Why can't I dedicate a year to taking care of me? With raised eyebrows, my friend replied, "Good luck with that."

However, as you stated in your book, the Universe gives back!

Maybe one day, our paths will cross, and I will tell you more.

GREAT BOOK! I hope it gives strength to many!

And her response:

Maggie ♥♥♥

Thank you for taking the time to message me.

Writing this book was one of the hardest things I have done. But as you know, no one understands what it is like, unless they have been through it.

I'm so proud and excited that you are taking 2018 to focus on you and heal ♥*. This is the key.*

Chapter Six | The Dinner, The Book

I would love for our paths to cross one day!!!
Enjoy Myrtle Beach

What author actually messages people who write to them? I had now experienced two authors that do.

I did meet that author at her book signing, we hugged, and our souls connected.

Two different normal everyday people, whose lives changed and inspired them to write about it.

Two everyday people whose books had landed in my hands at the right time, in the right place, to bring healing to my life. One author in Australia and this one in my very town! How freaking bizarre is that?

This book was pivotal in my healing. It was pivotal in teaching me a new way to love my child.

Tamara Arnold took a chance on being authentic, and lives are changed because of it. Her ripple has expanded to my world. Holy wow! How wild was this? Yet another ripple expands.

CHAPTER Seven

Death Doula

A Death Doula is a non-medical, caring, sensitive, and compassionate individual who has been trained to care for both the personal and emotional needs of the dying. Those approaching death have an individual journey they must travel. A Death Doula is a companion on that journey.

When going through the journey with my mom I remember telling the hospice team that I knew the experience would make me a better hospice volunteer. Little did I know what that would truly come to mean.

Little did I know at that time, I would come to find out what a Death Doula was. Little did I know at that time, I would take the training and become a Certified Death Doula myself.

A few months after my mom's death, I somehow heard about Death Doulas. I actually cannot even remember how that first came about, but I knew I was intrigued and interested. I began researching where to take the training, when someone, through hospice, connected me with training coming to my area. I felt the nudge to pursue this training.

I felt I was destined to train to companion the dying! I knew that my time volunteering with hospice was a treasured time in my life. The dying have so much to teach us. The dying, amongst other things, teach us how to live.

Chapter Seven | Death Doula

The dying had given so much more to me than I ever gave to them in my volunteer role.

Without hesitation, I signed up for the course and paid my fee. Wow! I really did this! Still grieving over the loss of my mom, who was I kidding? Yet the urging was greater than my apprehension, so I forged ahead.

On the morning of the first class, I was so nervous I felt sick. What if I broke down crying? What if it was too soon? What if, what if—the list went on. Fear is always there as we move into our destiny. Never let fear stand in the way of your dreams. Face the fear and crush it. Be mindful, pause, connect, and then send that fear on its way.

As I left the house and walked to the car that morning for the class, a cardinal flew right past my face, so close that I felt it. I smiled and thought, "Okay, Momma, I'm going."

I felt her presence with me that whole day.

On the second morning of the class, as I was driving down the highway, there, stuck in the bushes, was a huge bunch of balloons. I laughed out loud, for at my mom's memorial, we had a yard full of balloons because she had always said she hated funerals and funeral flowers, especially lilies. So instead, we had the yard full of mums and balloons. This morning those balloons were another reminder that she was still going with me.

Yes, I cried some, but it didn't even matter. I learned that part of being a good Death Doula is acknowledging your feelings and emotions.

I learned so much in that course and the subsequent training, and now, as a Certified Death Doula in 2019, I launched a practice called Whispers of Wisdom. I work hard now at living my passion and building awareness about death doulas. I hold regular "death cafés" to help increase awareness and have safe open spaces for dialogue on death and dying. I find that our culture tends to hide away death so much that even the dying cannot feel comfortable discussing it.

It is my belief that the more we have those difficult conversations in life, the less scary they become. I believe that about death conversations, mental health conversations, sexual assault, and the list goes on. It has been my life experience that when you shine the light in the darkness, it cannot remain dark.

Unfortunately, death is one of the absolutes of life. Every one of us will eventually die. I remember hearing in a documentary, *The End Game,* that you don't need to be friends with death, but you do need to have some type of relationship with it. That is so true.

Check me out at www.whispersofwisdom.ca. Where that journey leads, we are still finding out. What will grow out of it is left in the hands of Spirit.

CHAPTER

Letting The Wounds Speak

Sometimes we need to let go of the things we cannot fathom with our human understanding. Many things in this life will never make sense—stillborn babies, child abuse, world hunger, children dying, disease, animal abuse, terrorism, hate, and the list goes on and on. Some things will never make sense.

Instead of trying to make sense of the things that cause suffering, we need to quiet our minds and let those wounds and suffering speak. The sufferings in your life and in our world have something to teach us if we learn to take time to listen.

Pause and listen to the wound.

I tried for many years to understand a situation that caused a great wound to my children and me. I spent many sleepless nights trying to figure it out. How I could have prevented it, how I could have changed it, how I could heal it, how I could fix it, was it my fault, how had I caused it, why it was in our life? In all my efforts trying to figure it out, all I had done was to cause the wound to grow bigger in my life, to become infected over and over again, spill poison out onto others, and generally caused life to die

Chapter Eight | Letting The Wounds Speak

within and around me. Trying to make sense of it caused many bouts of anxiety and depression. Many times the depression was so vast, I could see only a sliver of light.

Did it change my circumstances? Absolutely not!

Did it heal the wound? Absolutely not!

Did I learn from it? I absolutely did! What I learned most was what *not* to do.

I learned not to dissect it. It won't change it, heal it, or fix it!

I learned to sit with the wound. Feel it, experience it, grieve it, and then move on from it. If you keep it, you make it part of you, you become victim to it, you wear it with you. Never let wounds define you.

Remember it as something that happened to you, it does not define you!

I learned that it only takes a spark of light to give someone hope.

I learned that there is no chasm so deep that I cannot find my way out.

I learned that there is always a way of escape.

The trouble is, that way of escape is rarely easy, and we need to do the work. Sometimes we need to let go of circumstances and people that are not good for our soul, and often that is extremely difficult. We often stay in the pit of hopelessness because it is our known place, it's familiar. Often we even feel deserving of our wounds.

I am here to tell you that this is a lie your mind tells you and wants you to believe. You were not created for suffering! You were created for greatness, to give and receive love.

Are you living with wounds that have become who you are? Sit with them, heal, and peel that off of your soul, because wounds are not part of your DNA, and the guilt that comes with those wounds will never serve you well. Let guilt go.

Since learning this lesson, I always remind people that guilt is the gift that keeps regifting to you, and that gift never becomes anything good. It's just wrapped in a different package, but it is still that same guilt. Let guilt go.

When we listen to the wounds, they will teach us valuable life lessons or love lessons on how to help others through a similar wound. There are few greater gifts of compassion and understanding that you can give another human than to be a beacon of light for them in their darkness.

You become that light by surviving your darkness!

Listen to your wounds, not for what they don't bring to your life, but for what greatness can come from those wounds. Let triumph come from tragedy!

Be the light! The world has enough darkness. Be *hope* in the darkness through the light of your healed life. Let your ripple expand to others.

CHAPTER
Nine

Walks With My Soul

I truly love walking or sitting with my soul. Early morning walks with my dog, Connor, always give me the freedom to connect with nature and my soul. That dog is never in a hurry. Always taking time to sniff every tree, bush, or anything else in his path. We should seek to take a lesson from our animals. They truly know the important things in life. As I saw on a pet store sign about how dogs handle stress, "If you can't eat it or play with it, pee on it, and walk away." Although we humans cannot go around peeing on things, we certainly can learn to walk away from whatever does not enrich our lives.

The birds fly freely without worry, never fearing if the branch they land on will hold the weight of their body. They sing without concern if anyone is even listening, or if

Chapter Nine | Walks With My Soul

the song is as good as the next bird's—just living free in their reality.

The trees stand proudly in all their glory, never fearing if the tree next to them is more beautiful or has a different purpose. Those that shed their foliage do so without worry about the change of life seasons. Yet we humans often get in a big tizzy when change comes to our life seasons. Often times, change brings good things, yet we fear change.

Why, then, do we, the more intelligent beings, live with worry, fretting over every little thing in our life? We are in a constant state of hurried hustle, planning every detail of life from birth to death. We are constantly busy and wonder why we suffer from anxiety and why our children are growing up with anxiety disorders.

We need to pause. Slow down. Get out in nature; learn lessons from nature. Schedule time to walk with your soul. Invite Spirit on that walk, you may be surprised at what you see and hear. You might be surprised at all the gifts the Universe has to share with you.

I was invited to go on a cruise with a friend a few years ago. I found that I loved cruising, but not for the excitement of the exotic ports of call. I found that I really liked time on the ship, cut off from the outside world, especially on the private balcony. I would wake up very early as the sun was rising and sit out there for hours, just looking at the vastness of the ocean. The wonder of the ocean. On a few occasions, I would have the pleasure of a private dolphin show. Or so I thought, but not really, because the dolphins were oblivious to my presence. They were swimming for enjoyment, playfully jumping in that moment of time.

They, too, knew the secret of their existence: the call of nature to exist only in who they were meant to be.

When you slow down and walk with your soul, you, too, can find the secret to your existence—the fact that it really is no secret at all. The Universe freely gives knowledge to all. So seek knowledge, and you will find it.

I invite and challenge you to go on walks with your soul. Get out in nature and quiet your mind so your soul can speak. In those walks, you will find wisdom, clarity, peace, gratitude, calm, serenity, and a vast array of other gifts just waiting to be found.

CHAPTER

Moments With Higher Self

When I pause, connect, and be mindful, I can and often do connect with my Higher Self. My Higher Self is pure soul without ego, only seeking my highest and best self.

When you face difficult life challenges, ask your Higher Self for divine guidance. I recall circumstances in my journey where wisdom and solutions were beyond my understanding or grasp. Someone once told me just to ask my Higher Self. I wondered, do I have a Higher Self? You bet I do, we all do!

Higher Self imparts wisdom, by taking ego out of the circumstance. When the emotional responses to a wound are gone (ego), love can heal, even without understanding.

My Higher Self is non-judgmental of both myself and others. My Higher Self is neutral, with only my highest good as its intention! It's hard to imagine my highest good as the intention. That means, not my comfort zone as the intention, not my feelings as the intention, not equality as the intention, not fairness as the intention, and not my wishes as the intention. Holy wow! Think about the power in that! My highest good is the only intention!

Chapter Ten | Moments With Higher Self

Talk about the Universe having your back! That Higher Self has your top, bottom, and sides, past, present, and future covered—your consistent go-to source!

It was in one of those Higher Self moments that I learned when I heal myself, I also heal my past generations as well as future generations. That was a pivotal (a-ha) moment for me.

I can recall on a few occasions where I would lay in the darkness on my bed and look to my Higher Self above me as a shining aura in the darkness with a stream of wisdom pouring into my being.

I have walked with her through some difficult times in my life. I'm sure there are a few people still alive today because of the wisdom of my Higher Self. (Haha!)

I encourage you to find that connection with your Higher Self, and start the daily dialogue as you gain wisdom and insights for life.

Remember, Higher Self only operates in love, never with judgment, never through guilt, and never in shame. If you feel those, it's a counterfeit! Seek Higher Self wisdom.

CHAPTER

Eleven

The Gifts On The Porch

Although I have always had a deep personal faith in God, I have also encountered and experienced many of the gifts that I believe were left on my porch on that dream walk. I list and give links to a few here, but invite you to seek yours by asking Spirit for *your* healing journey. All of these different modalities found me; I did not go in search of them.

I am equally sure that there are still many more, yet-hidden gifts, to be revealed in divine timing on my journey.

I invite you to look beyond the possibilities that now reside within your mind and be open to the infinite wonder yet to be revealed. I invite you to be open to the possibility that there is much more out there than what our minds presently comprehend. Could there be more wisdom than you presently feel and understand?

Aqualead

Aqualead is a new energy that heals water in living beings and in the environment. It was channeled by Sabine Blais on August 30, 2018, in Buenos Aires, Argentina.

http://aqualeadinstitute.org/

Chapter Eleven | The Gifts On The Porch

Aromatherapy

Aromatherapy is a holistic healing treatment that uses natural plant extracts to promote health and well-being.

https://www.healthline.com/health/what-is-aromatherapy

Mindfulness

Mindfulness is maintaining a moment-by-moment awareness of our thoughts, feelings, body sensations, and the surrounding environment through a gentle, nurturing lens.

https://greatergood.berkeley.edu/topic/mindfulness/definition

http://mindfullymad.org/

Meditation

Meditation is a means of transforming the mind.

https://www.gaiam.com/blogs/discover/meditation-101-techniques-benefits-and-a-beginner-s-how-to

Ho'oponopono

Ho'oponopono is the Hawaiian practice of reconciliation and forgiveness. It includes the mantra, "I love you, I'm sorry, please forgive me, and thank you." The word Ho'Oponopono translated to English means "to make right." Therapist Dr. Haleaka Hew Len, Ph.D., used this method of healing therapy to cure an entire ward of criminally insane patients without ever seeing any of them. There are many avenues to find out about this Hawaiian practice, I include just one.

https://upliftconnect.com/hawaiian-practice-of-forgiveness/

Reiki

Reiki is a Japanese technique for stress reduction and relaxation that also promotes healing. The word Reiki is made up of two Japanese words—Rei, which means "God's wisdom or the Higher Power," and Ki which is "life force energy."

https://www.reiki.org/faqs/what-reiki

https://iarp.org/how-does-reiki-work/

Therapeutic Touch

Therapeutic Touch is a modern application of ancient forms of healing that uses the laying-on-of-hands, with the practitioner using his or her hand in the client's energy field to bring that field into balance and harmony.

https://therapeutictouch.org/

Grief Support

Grief Support is "holding space" with someone in their grief. It is not fixing it, making it go away, or taking them out of it. It is compassionately being a companion to the client or friend.

https://www.hellogrief.org

Synchronization

Synchronization is the coordination of events or the process of allowing threads to execute one after the other the existence of relation to one another.

Chapter Eleven | The Gifts On The Porch

https://www.gaia.com/article/synchronicity-not-just-coincidence

Intuition

Intuition is a process that gives us the ability to know something without analytic reasoning, bridging the gap between the conscious and the unconscious parts of our mind.

https://en.wikipedia.org/wiki/Intuition

Psychic Ability

A psychic is a person who professes the ability to perceive information hidden from the normal senses through extrasensory perception (ESP), or is said by others to have such abilities.

https://en.wikipedia.org/wiki/List_of_psychic_abilities

Crystals

Proponents of this technique believe that crystals act as conduits for healing—allowing positive healing energy to flow into the body as negative, disease-causing energy flows out.

https://www.livescience.com/40347-crystal-healing.html

https://time.com/4969680/do-crystals-work/

Nature Therapy

Nature Therapy is the use of time in nature to ground and heal. The energy properties in nature can be a source of calm healing.

https://www.natureandforesttherapy.org/

CHAPTER Twelve

My First Speaking Engagement

It was December 26, 2018, and we were celebrating Christmas as a family.

Early that morning, I had a vision of an eagle. The eagle was flying over my house and hovering just above the roof. I watched as healing oils ran down the wings, onto my roof down the sides of the walls, and flowed under my dining room table. I heard, "Let the oil heal your family." It was powerful and spoke to my soul. I prepared for the day, never telling anyone about the vision or how it gave me strength.

My children and their partners, along with my sister and her family, came over and we all celebrated together. We laughed together, chatted together, and had the best Christmas we have had in many years. It was a truly beautiful day. I was so thankful and felt the power in that vision. I felt the healing. Still, I pondered the vision. Was it real, or was it just my dreams of reality?

About 370 miles and six hours away, another mom was having Christmas with her family on that same December 26th day. Spirit told her that day to post a call-out for speakers for a women's retreat she was planning for

Chapter Twelve | My First Speaking Engagement

International Woman's Day in March. She listened and made the post before she went to bed.

The next day, early in the morning, I got an email from my friend and mentor, Songbird, sending me the "call for speakers" email and expressing to me that she felt I needed to go. I told her I thought it would be fun to go, to which she said something to the effect of, "No, you don't understand. I believe you are supposed to speak there."

I ask her if she was crazy or drinking very early in the morning. I had never spoken at a women's retreat, and I was pretty sure that they would be looking for experienced speakers with something of value to say. We argued back and forth for a bit, but in the end, just to humor her, I told her to go ahead and submit my name and see what happens, never thinking anything would come of it.

A bit later, she messaged me and said that she couldn't find the email, and I would have to do it myself. Again, to humor her, I filled in the online form and submitted it, later finding out that was her plan all along. A wise woman she may have been.

Within a few minutes of hitting send, my telephone rang—it was the organizer asking if I had time to speak with her about my submission. Long story short, before long in that conversation, I heard myself agreeing to speak at her conference.

Was I crazy, I had not even looked up to see where this place was? It was over six hours to the north, and I had just agreed to go there in the heart of winter. What was I thinking?

I immediately called Songbird, telling her that if she got me into this, the least she could do was to come along. She agreed as well, without checking to see how far away it was either.

So here I was, a few months from speaking at my first women's conference with no idea what to speak about. All I knew was that the theme of the conference was "Finding Balance."

I was in a state of panic, struggling with the magnitude of what I had agreed to do. Finally, one night before bed, I had a conversation with Spirit. You see, I talk to my soul just as I speak to a friend—the kind of friend who knows my deepest fears but loves me anyway. That friend. The gist of that conversation was me recognizing that I did have a story to tell if I could just be brave enough to tell it. I asked my Creator and spirit guides to help me write something. Spirit responded at about 3:00 a.m., as sometimes happens because we often don't slow down long enough in our waking hours to listen. At least for me, sleep time is when Spirit likes to talk with me.

The following script on Balance is what Spirit woke me up in the early hours of the morning to write.

I didn't know it yet, but this book was already in the works as Spirit had a plan in motion. Synchronicity was at work yet again in my life, or should I say, is always at work in my life—and yours as well, by the way.

Like Japanese *kintsugi* (kin-sugi), the art of mending broken pottery using gold makes a broken piece more valuable than before it was damaged.

Chapter Twelve | My First Speaking Engagement

Soul healing mends the broken parts of our soul and creates something beautiful out of the traumas of our lives. Soul healing is the process of mending from the inside out.

When we are broken, we cover up the damages to our soul using many masks, some so good we even fool ourselves. Then one day, something causes our mask to fall, or we decide we want to live an authentic life and choose to remove our mask.

This is the acronym I believe that Spirit gave me for *balance*.

Be you.

Authentic self. Be your authentic self. Not the mask you live behind, whatever that may be to you. You know your mask intimately. Mine was "the strong one," the one who would be everything to everyone except me. The go-to person. Always in control. But behind the mask, was the authentic me. The one who never felt worthy, the emotional train wreck, quick to anger, with my identity wrapped up in my work and what others thought of me. I securely kept that mask in place, rarely being my authentic self. It is so wonderfully freeing to let the mask go. I can love unconditionally without the mask, be my authentic self without the worry of being accepted. I accept me, and that is enough.

Love yourself first, love others next. We think it is selfish to put ourselves to the top of the list, but if we fill our cup first, we feed others with the overflowing cup. If we love from an empty cup, we feed others with the dry bits left from the bottom of the well, from the sediment. And then we wonder why they can't receive our love. Why it is not nourishing to their soul. No, because it's the waste from the bottom of our empty cup. When your cup is full, and your soul is nourished, love comes naturally from your being. Strangers are drawn to it. Your friends and family notice that your whole countenance has changed. Love overflows.

Align yourself to your spirit path. You know that path, deep in your gut, that place you feel free. That Higher Self! Meditate on that. If you don't know your path, seek it. Ask your spirit guides to show you. They will. I am living proof in the flesh that when you align yourself to Spirit, they show up. On your front porch, in the car, in the voice of strangers, in meditation, in messages, in dreams, in nature, trust me, they show up.

Notice your emotions, do they serve you, do they control you, do they rule your life? Remember, emotions come and go like the waves in the ocean. Sometimes they beat you under, and other times they lift you up for the ride of your life. They are a constant shift. Don't put your faith in something constantly shifting. When emotions come, recognize them, acknowledge them, learn from them, and then let them go.

Calm yourself, quiet your mind, close off the head noise, stress noise, negative noise. For me, meditation does this, being at the water does this, being out in nature does this, listening to the birds does this, sipping a beautiful cup of coffee does this, holding my dog close does this, breathing does this. When I first tried meditation, all it consisted of was the breathing exercise: "Breathe in, *I am*—breathe out, *at peace*." Four small words would calm

Chapter Twelve | My First Speaking Engagement

my headspace. Over and over, I practiced just that. At first, it took a long time for calm to come, but now, I can summon that calm sometimes in a single breath.

Enjoy life. Live each day with gratitude. Gratitude is a seed that spreads itself, kind of like a mint plant. You plant one of those little suckers, and before you know it, your garden is full of mint. When you wake up every day thanking the sun for coming up, thankful for breath, thankful for a place to wake up, you start to notice other things in your day to be thankful for. Simple things we take for granted and don't even notice. Like freshly-brewed coffee, a bird singing, the laughter of a baby, your puppy greeting you at the door, a flower in the garden, a heart-shaped rock in your path, a feather in your path, the simple things that are free to everyone—except the coffee, that's not free. So much of life we take for granted or miss in the busy lives we choose. Slow down, enjoy the journey.

At that conference, I shared that I was like that kintsugi bowl. Lives torn apart by tragic circumstances mended together by the gold of my Creator, angels, the Universe, spirit guides, and possibly even my sweet momma. That acronym was not just for the women at the conference, it was a message for me to share with the world.

I had been invited by Spirit to come to Northern Ontario to be a beacon of light and hope to the women sitting before me at that conference. It was the beginning of me sharing my truth. Was I up to that task? Although I wasn't sure about that, I knew all I could be was the authentic Maggie that I had learned to become, just as I had when I became a single parent with wounded children and I knew I had a decision to make—turn tragedy into victory or just stay where I was. I knew back then that my children had a better chance of surviving our mess if I got back up and began the climb out of my darkness. I knew now that I can be a beacon of light in a dark world if I continue to be authentically brave.

Spirit obviously believed that my story could be that beacon of light to someone in their personal dark valley, and I fully believed that someone at this conference needed to know there was hope.

I told them that I would like to say that the climb up was full of butterflies and buttercups, but that was far from the truth. It was dirty and messy most of the time. Many times I did things right, but just as many times, I completely got it wrong. I messed up probably more than I got it right. I don't think anyone climbing out of the darkness does it without getting some torn up knees as well as scrapes and bruises. As humans (and mothers), we are, most of the time, less than perfect. The key is to keep going. When you fall, get back up and keep going. Life is a constant learning curve, and most of life's tragic curves do not come with an instruction manual for navigating the way out. I certainly knew that I did not get the "How to be a Good Mother" manual.

I learned in this journey that I cannot fix or heal anyone, even my own children. I can take them to the place of healing, I can be a role model of healing, but they themselves must choose to heal.

I don't want to tell their story, but suffice to say, my children both grew into adult lives with deep childhood

Chapter Twelve | My First Speaking Engagement

wounds. Some scars so deep, they continue to break open. Some scars have healed with bacteria inside that need to open, be cleaned out for true healing to come. But heal they can. In any circumstance, we can all heal.

I told those women at the conference that if anyone was suffering with a teenage runaway, suffering from physical abuse, mental abuse, cutting, alcohol abuse, fear of suicide, in and out of rehab, I understood their pain!

If you are wondering if your loved one will ever feel freedom from suffering, I understand your pain!

I told them and tell you today, you can love and support your loved one, but you cannot heal them. Only they can choose healing. That is a tough reality to face!

I shared about the countless times I cried out to God as a weary mom, not knowing what else to do. I told them about one day in the depths of my fear and brokenness, crying in the shower. It had been close to a year since my daughter ran away from the group home; my baby was somewhere in the USA running from her brokenness. I had no idea where she was or if she was safe. I was pretty sure she was not safe. My greatest fear since she ran away was that I would get that call. You know the call—the one where someone gives you the worst news of your life. The one where you find out your child is never coming home. I knew I needed to face that fear head-on if this mom was ever going to heal.

I shared with the women about hearing a voice in my Spirit that day in the shower. It said: "Give the child back to me, give her back to the one who loves her more than you do, give her to me and leave her there."

I knew that this was what I had to do. This is a place no mother wants to go, but if you're there, I understand your pain!

I shared with those women at the conference the raw, authentic side of myself and empowered them by offering them a light in their darkness.

Just as the mother bird pushes the baby birds to fly, we must nudge each other to fly. Spirit has brought us together to encourage one another to soar! Before we can soar, we must heal! Commit to healing.

I shared with them that as we heal ourselves, we fill our cup, our cup overflows and causes a ripple effect which will spread far beyond and heal further than we can even imagine.

I encouraged them to find healing, no matter how long it takes. I think for me, although I searched for healing the whole time, I never got it because I was too busy serving/taking care of others. Hospice has a mandatory time off after a personal loss. What a gift that time was for me. I had never given myself permission to heal, let alone any personal healing time after any of my life losses. It was always get up, brush off, suck it up, and move on. That year of healing was the greatest gift I had ever given myself.

The balance theme at this conference was the key. I encouraged them to give themselves permission. Permission to heal, take that healing time, don't put on the wrong mask, and don't pour from the empty cup.

Maybe that was the light bulb message in this! I realized the significance of it that day.

Chapter Twelve | My First Speaking Engagement

Just as flight attendants warn at the beginning of every flight, "Put on your own oxygen mask first," I put on the wrong mask years ago. Bam! I learned a valuable life lesson.

Do you mask up with the healing, life-sustaining mask or the mask of covering your pain? Holy cow! Eighteen years later, I found out I should have put on my oxygen mask first! God, I wish I had known back then! But I know now and encourage you to put your mask on *first*!

The impact of my being authentic and real with those women was powerful. It took my breath away! Not only had Spirit orchestrated my being a light to one person at that conference, but there were also many tissues being passed around that afternoon.

My authentic life of finding my soul had touched the heart of many women in the room that day. Several women came to me after to express gratitude for my being a light. My being authentic and open and bringing light in my darkness had given them the safe space to be open about their own darkness.

If you are reading my words today and your soul is living in your personal darkness, I offer you that same light. The light of healing out of that darkness is available to you as well. Give yourself permission to find that healing. Let go of guilt and shame, and know that you are truly loved by your soul's Creator.

As I was writing this chapter, my phone rang again, yes, my daughter. Just wanting to chat with her momma, and with tears in my eyes and a lump in my throat, I remind you again that healing is possible. Just as I shared with the women at the conference, I share with you. Never give up! Never give up on your soul healing.

That call reminded me of another call I got from her from the new group home. This call came from Florida, where Spirit had asked the help of another stranger to get my baby off the streets. You know how it's said that cats have nine lives, well so does my daughter, and she has used quite a few. Do I believe in miracles, you ask? You bet I do! That call was close to another Christmas I will never forget. As Christmas approached that year, she was missing. I was still buying little presents for her, and when she called, I asked if I could send them to her. On that Christmas morning, they allowed her to call me collect, and I heard her tell me that since she arrived at the home, she had started a list of things she needed and kept it by her bed. In the box that I had sent her was everything on her list. Do I believe in miracles, you ask? You bet I do! You see, that same Spirit that asked me to give my child over to the one who loved her more than I did had allowed this mother the gift of giving her those things on the list. Could anyone have supplied those few things she needed? You bet, but the gift to me was that I did. I believe in miracles, and so can you.

Do we have it all together? Not by a long shot. Do I always make the right decisions? Not by a long shot. As a human being, I sometimes sabotage myself as much as the next person, and when I do, I forgive myself, love myself anyway, and carry on.

I invite you to do the same. Love is your superpower! Love for yourself. Love for others. It's the only superpower you will ever need.

CHAPTER

Thirteen

The Changed Maggie – Without The Mask

The song *I Can See Clearly Now* by Johnny Nash comes into my mind as I start to write this chapter. Those words are my new reality.

Those words ring true for my life recollection; my darkness blinded me to any hope that was around me. I was a wounded, angry mother trying to raise two beautiful children to be well-healed humans. Who was I kidding? How could I ever think I could do that when my own wounds were so deep as to fundamentally change me forever? I did the best I could with the knowledge I had at that time. They did grow into beautiful adults, still healing.

One of my favorite quotes from Maya Angelou is, "Do the best you can until you know better. Then, when you know better, do better." There is such wisdom in that.

How can we do better until we know better? Yet, we continue to guilt ourselves for our imperfections and lack of knowledge.

Chapter Thirteen | The Changed Maggie Without The Mask

For at least 20 years of my life, I had carried so much anger, guilt, shame, and bitterness that it ate deep into my core. Oh, I was still a good person, but with it, I carried an angry edge of deep pain that continued to build the walls of self-preservation I believed I needed to survive. How could I love others until I learned how to love Maggie?

I had worn my masks for so many years, I had no idea who the authentic me was. Those masks I wore covered the deep wounds that were like a poison to my soul. Yes, I was a good mother, organized, successful in my job, a pillar of strength to anyone who needed me. Yet on the inside was such a deeply wounded soul. A soul without hope and full of sadness. A soul who felt unworthy of love.

If you are that person, let me assure you that you can find your way out of that sadness. That angry, bitter person is not who you are! You were created to receive and give love!

You are loved and worthy of being loved.

If you don't like the path you are on, choose another! Every day that you wake up alive is a chance to start over. Choose a new reality. Seek out the help of professionals if you need to. Seek out wisdom. There are many examples or paths to choose as a starting point in this little book, but the most important is the decision to change.

Healing is like peeling off the layers of an onion. Bit by bit, you peel away at the limiting beliefs building on the new truths as you find your healing. Make it your quest. Your personal journey to your soul.

Start with some short guided meditations. Don't worry if your mind wanders, even those seasoned in meditation run into that. Simply return your focus to your breath and start again. When I began to meditate, I used four little words: "I am at peace." Breathe in, *I am*—breathe out, *at peace*. A simple little meditation that, in the beginning, was so difficult for me. I practiced it over and over. With practice, came calm. Now I can quiet a raging storm with those four little words. If I can, so can you.

Start with a little self-care, which is more than what I thought it was. It's more than just a quick alone time in the shower. Learn what makes you happy; learn what ignites the passion in your soul. The internet is full of self-care ideas. Find a few and start somewhere. Take care of *you*!

I can truly say that I now live the authentic Maggie life. No more masks, guilt, or shame. I love and accept myself, imperfect human that I am. I do the best I can to follow my path, and validation from others, although sometimes great, is not necessary. I have found through my healing that *I am enough*. I do my best to live each day as it comes, being mindful, and continuing to heal and grow in my journey. When I stumble or fall, I get back up and keep going.

Probably one of the most profound things that I have learned over the last few years besides being my authentic self is this:

I am a soul living a human experience and not the other way around.

I truly love you and speak blessing and hope into your being.

CHAPTER Fourteen

The Vision, The Vibration, The Village

My vision is to give and receive love fully.

My vision is to increase my vibration with my Creator in such a way that it brings hope to others and guides them to their journey to soul.

My vision is to be the village and to create a village of love. To encourage people to love each other a little more. To spend the rest of my life living from my soul, so connected to the Universe that I can be a light in the darkness—a little spark to ignite the fire in others who may have lost their light.

My vision is to keep the ripple flowing for the rest of my days in this life.

Thank you for your commitment to reading my book.

I hope it inspires you to find your journey to the soul if you haven't already.

But most of all, I hope you know that you are loved!

Chapter Fourteen | The Vision, The Vibration, The Villiage

In love and light,

Maggie ♥

P.S. I'm also that author you can reach out to. You can reach me through my Facebook page, Maggie Morris, or at info@whispersofwisdom.ca.

CHAPTER Fifteen

Soul Whispers From Maggie

The following are journal posts pulled from the last year to share my journey to soul with you. Be inspired to be you!

Mindfulness

Mindfulness
I must be authentic
I always need to work at this!
Learning to let the emotions just be
And *not* create a story
A story my brain will replay
When I least expect it
When I am too weak to realize
That it is a story
Created from an emotion
Possibly
Likely
Not my reality
But a story
Created from an emotion
Created from a triggering memory
Created from a wound
One tiny emotion

Chapter Fifteen | Soul Whispers From Maggie

Created a story
We now believe
Mindfulness eliminates the story
Mindfulness allows the emotion
Without the story
Pause, connect, be mindful ♥

The Journey

The journey isn't about
Becoming a different person
But loving who you are
Right now!

I have been lying here quietly for more than an hour
Listening to the wind
Contemplating a busy day ahead
Being thankful and
Cuddling with my puppy
Perfectly contented!
Accepting of myself
Imperfections and all
Happily encouraging others
To love themselves
Accept themselves
Be kind to themselves
For in that we find
The secret to our happiness
It has been there all along
Love + Acceptance + Kindness = Happiness

Just for Today
Just for today,
Truly love yourself
Just for today,
Truly accept yourself
Just for today,
Truly be kind to yourself
When negativity creeps in
Give it a halt, and
Tell it
Just for today,
I love myself
I accept myself
I am kind to myself

And tomorrow
Repeat
Until it sinks deep into your being!
In love and light

The Wound

Let it hurt
Let it bleed
Let it heal
Let it go

To that wound
That keeps surfacing
I love you, please forgive me, I'm sorry, thank you
Thank you
For reminding me

Chapter Fifteen | Soul Whispers From Maggie

That I am a soul in a human
And as humans
Sometimes we pick up
That which we had already let go

If you can understand and relate
Let me remind you
You are not your thoughts
You are a soul within a human
Forgive yourself and let it go again ♥

What I Owe

You don't owe anyone
Anything except
The same amount
Of respect
They show you!

To be authentic, I will admit I used to believe this

Now it breaks my heart
I love you, I'm sorry, please forgive me, thank you
Why?

Because we *owe* everyone love
Because we *owe* everyone respect
Especially those that have not loved or respected us
We are called to love
Remembering that those who disrespect, hurt, and wound
Do so from their woundedness

Journey To Soul

Trust me, my authentic self
Understands the effort required
To love when you want to hate
To forgive requires sacrifice

And to my core, I believe
The statement below should read:

You owe everyone
Much more
Love and respect
Than they have
Been able to show you

That statement has the ability
To both increase your vibration
And change your world! ♥

Dip In

"Dip into your soul
Find your truth
What calls to your heart
What moves your spirit
Make your life dance
To the song of your essence!"

I dipped
Now I sing to my essence
Your approval, not required
I sing to my soul essence

Chapter Fifteen | Soul Whispers From Maggie

Love is the music
She has found her peace
Within her soul

Find yours, look within
You will be amazed. ♥

Finding Peace

I find my peace within
Everything else falls
Into place

How I found *my* peace
Go within
To find your peace
Clean
Declutter
Let go
It's there
Inside yourself
Find it
Find your true value ♥

The Soul

Every soul is whole
No matter
How wounded
The mind is
My soul smiles at this
It says

You understand now
You are not wounded
Your mind is wounded
You are not broken
Your mind is broken
You are not tired
Your mind is tired

Your soul is well
It is your mind
Seeking wholeness
Look to your soul
Heal your mind ♥

Triggered Wounds

In any given moment
I might be wounded
But I can choose
Not to act from my wound

I have experienced
That we can be triggered by old wounds
Something may come up
And you feel the sting
We are shocked
And think, "I let that go already"
Guilt and anxiety arises
But be reminded, my friend
It is simply the sting of the memory
The wound is not back

Chapter Fifteen | Soul Whispers From Maggie

Just the memory
Do not fear a memory
Happy memories
Come and go
We don't fear
When triggered by the memory of a wound
Let it simply come and go
Show gratitude for the memory
For in the memory
You remember the lesson
For in the memory
Remember you survived
To thrive ♥

One Day

And then it happens
You wake up one day
And everything falls into place
Your heart is calm
Your soul is lit

I am so
Thankful
Grateful
Blessed
I found this place
Within me
When I removed
The clutter
The pain

When I allowed
Forgiveness
When love
Replaced
Judgment
The light of your soul
Shines on *you*
And you *see*
Truly see her ♥

The Magic of Your Soul

You do not need
To believe in magic
You are magic
Believe in yourself!

Close your eyes
Feel the magic
Of your soul
The innocence
Of your soul
The purity
Of your soul
The love
Of your soul
Love yourself
Let the magic rise ♥

Values

Your values are defined

Chapter Fifteen | Soul Whispers From Maggie

By what is most important
In your life

What is shaping your decisions?
Don't like your life
Change your values
Your life will align

What you value
Drives your purpose
What you value
Feeds your passion

Is what you value
Feeding your soul or your ego?
Look within
Let love be your guide, not judgment ♥

My New Job

Sending love
Wherever it's needed

My new job!
My mission in life
Simply put

To the sick
To the wounded
To the heartbroken
To the tired

To the suffering
To those without hope
I cannot fix, cure, or heal
But I can love
And in love, there is healing ♥

The View

The view from my bed.

The view from my bed—these trees speak wisdom, sometimes fairies dance there, sometimes in the wind, they show me visions and send me messages as I meditate with gratitude for a new day!

Even today, as I awoke with a pounding headache and a cry in my heart, they speak of stillness, and as I look, I see the door reminding us to be still in turmoil, be still and wait for wisdom. The wisdom does not come in the turmoil of life, it comes in the stillness of our mind.

If you are in turmoil today, wisdom says this:
Be still, my child, be still
For in the stillness, I come
Quiet the mind with stillness
Quiet the mind with love
For in the stillness peace comes
For in the stillness worry leaves
For in the stillness fear leaves
For in the stillness anxiety leaves
In the stillness breathe

Chapter Fifteen | Soul Whispers From Maggie

I love you
I'm sorry
Please forgive me
Thank you
In the stillness, peace comes ♥

The Darkness

In the darkness

When life brings in a deep grieving darkness
And you cannot see the light
I will look for light
I will send you light

When life brings in a deep grieving darkness
I will hold space for you
With my light
Look for my light

When life brings in a deep grieving darkness
I will not judge your grief
I will not fix your grief
I will hold space for you
Until you see your light again

In your darkness, I am there

Written with much love, to my hurting friend ♥

Peace

I am peace
Or
I am turmoil
That choice is completely up to me

Think about that

I choose peace! ♥

The Authentic Life

Peace comes when you live an authentic life, the pressures of fitting in and being who others think you should be fall away when you truly find who you are.

Be you, that's the best you can be.

Let your opinion of you be the only opinion that matters!

Live the life you love and love the life you live! ♥

Ho'oponopono

Today
I would say I love you, I'm sorry, please forgive me, thank you.

Ten years ago
I was taking care of everyone (the best I could), except me.
I am taking care of me, I am

Chapter Fifteen | Soul Whispers From Maggie

I was angry, hurt, broken, and wounded
I am healed, I am
I was without hope
I am hope, I am
I was hiding behind the mask
I am free, I am
I was living behind the veil
I am open, I am
I was looking together
I am me, I am
I was anything but together
I am whole, I am
I was not authentic
I am authentic, I am

If you are wounded
I love you, I'm sorry, please forgive me, thank you.

You can find your authentic self!

Do you know what makes your soul shine?
Do you know what makes you happy?
Do you know what brings you peace?
Do you know calm tranquility?
Do you know your value?

If you answered no to any of these questions, go on a discovery to find your true authentic higher self, and you will be able to turn the no to yes.

I love you, I'm sorry, please forgive me, thank you

My Truth

My truth
I must be my truth
Because
I am healed
I am inspiring
I am authentic
I do attract beautiful souls
I do vibrate high
I do attract what I want
And
I *am* the ripple! ♥

Roots Exposed

Roots exposed
Sometimes in life, we feel exposed.
Sometimes in life, our pain is exposed.
Sometimes in life, we don't see the roots
But in this image we do
Just imagine the growth below the surface
Just imagine your growth beyond your circumstance
Just imagine the growth within your circumstance
Just imagine the power in the roots
From those roots, new life
From those roots, healing
From those roots, generations grow

Just imagine your roots expanding
In love and healing ♥

Chapter Fifteen | Soul Whispers From Maggie

Peace

Finding peace
This is how I achieved peace!
Not concerning myself
With what others think
About who I am
But, being who I am
Not what I think I am
But what I am
My authentic Maggie! ♥

It Takes One

All it takes
Is one person
In any generation
To heal
A family's
Limiting beliefs

I believe this
I awoke with this on my mind at about 5:00 a.m. today
I realize now
That I implanted many limiting beliefs in my children
Some created by me
Some implanted on me
Today
I release them from those limiting beliefs
I release my ancestors from their limiting beliefs
I release my future generations from those limiting beliefs
I replace those limiting beliefs with

Empowering beliefs
Hope
Truth
Faith
Love
Knowledge
Knowing
Intuition
Power
Wisdom
Gratitude
But the greatest of these is love! ♥

Look Carefully

"Things are not always as they seem."
The message I awoke to this morning

Eleven months ago, I lost my job!
Awful, right?
Or wonderful??
That job
Was unfulfilling
The owners unkind
It increased my blood pressure
Was not in line with my values
So what some may see as awful
In reality, was really wonderful

I have had the best year of my life
Growing as a person

Chapter Fifteen | Soul Whispers From Maggie

Understanding me
Finding me
Healing me
Finding *my* passion
Linking up with like-minded people
Listening to my heart and soul

If you find yourself struggling with something awful,
Look carefully at your situation.
Because sometimes something wonderful is packaged in awful wrapping
Sometimes you need to take time in the unwrapping to find the true gift!

Be thankful for what the Universe removes from your life.
Sometimes you need it gone, but lack the courage to remove it yourself

Look for the blessings in your "awful."

Love and light, my friends

Ignite the Flame

Something is brewing
In my heart and mind
Empowering those
Who have forgotten their value
Forgotten their flame
Forgotten their ripple

Ignite the flame

Start the ripple
Ignited by spirit
From my heart to yours
From yours to another
Change our world
With a single spark
With a single ripple

Are you in?
Can you hear it calling?

Be Your Miracle

I woke up at 4:00 a.m.
Watched a movie
At the end, Spirit gave me a valuable message
For me
And for others

Every day you wake up
And have a second chance
To do whatever you want
To be whoever you want
The only thing stopping you
Is you!

Be empowered (by empowering others)
Be courageous (though shy)
Be authentic (the real you is worth the effort)
Be fearless (even when you're scared)
Listen to your inner calling and believe in miracles. Be your miracle!

Chapter Fifteen | Soul Whispers From Maggie

The Place

There is this place
Inside you
Where nothing is impossible
Seek that

Childs Play

Inner child play

My inner child had so much fun today in St. Jacob's with two beautiful women in my life!

I felt the excitement of that inner child with each new treasure, but what I treasure most are the people Spirit brings into my life!

I am blessed! I am thankful, grateful, and amazed at how rich my life is!

I encourage everyone to live your authentic life, heal yourself, love yourself, forgive yourself, and live your passion.

If you need help to figure that out, ask the Universe to place people in your life to grow you and remove people from your life that inhibit your personal growth.

As we all live with authenticity and love ourselves, we cause a ripple of love that touches the lives of others and propels change in our world. ♥

Eagle Healing

Healing
I posted this yesterday
But today, it sinks deep into my consciousness!
The eagle pours healing over me to bring healing to others,
Past, present, future
Powerful truth!
Wow!
This is why we must all strive to find our individual healing!
I heal for my ancestors
I heal for my children
I heal for my grandchildren
I heal for my great-grandchildren
What powerful truth will be rooted in them? ♥

Purpose

Love

Maggie, your purpose
Is to give love
To those who need it
You have already
Experienced being denied
The love you deserve
You simply couldn't bear
To see others
Go through the same thing

Chapter Fifteen | Soul Whispers From Maggie

The Brew

My authentic self speaks again

I never intended to be one
The one who blamed others for my anger and rage
For fifteen years (or longer) it grew in me
The bubbling cauldron
Like a witches brew
Every wrong, every wound
Into the pot it went
Growing bigger and bigger
With each passing day
Boiling over, burning others, wounding others

Then one day I decided
To change the recipe

Into my pot I poured
Self-love, self-forgiveness, self-grace,
Self-acceptance, self-care with a hint of blessing
I watched over time
As love grew it healed old wounds
Self-forgiveness grew into forgiving others
Grace and acceptance became the mirror
To give grace and acceptance to others
Self-care healed and changed the caldron
Into a beautiful waterfall
And that hint of blessing
Became stars of gratitude
Shining to the wounded
A beacon of hope

Living proof
Change your life, change your world
Pause, connect, be mindful ♥

One Day

"Tell the story of the mountain you climbed.
Your words could become a page
to someone else's survival guide." Morgan Harper Nichols

You matter!

The Power of Yet

My authentic self.
Last night I went to a dreamcatcher making class, I know, I'm just as shocked as you!
Every part of my earth-self was in "flee" mode.
The recording playing over in my head was, "What the hell were you thinking signing up for this?"
The instructor, at one point, jokingly said, "You're supposed to smile and have fun doing this."
But, she was unaware of the raging war within my being.
I so wanted to make one, but my limited beliefs were causing me to want to flee.
Telling me the story of all my unsuccessful attempts to be crafty.
I think crafty
I dream crafty
But do crafty—that gift has eluded me. I was not crafty *yet*.

The power of "yet" came into my life this week, for this night.
I stayed, laughed, even swore a bit, but in the end, completed the masterpiece.
It may not have the value of a rare piece of art,
But to me, it holds a valuable lesson.
My limiting beliefs do not control my life choices, I do.
I can rise above my fears
Maybe this was not as easy for me as a "crafty" person
But I did not let the fear of failure cause me to give up.
Keep striving.
Never give up.
Even if you are just not there yet.

True Colors

True colors
I strive to be authentic
My true self
Loving all
Giving all
Being my best self
Allowing my true colors
To always be my truth
Because
I serve others
At no benefit to me
Except *love* ♥

Be the Light

Be the light

It is my goal
It is my passion
To hold space
To hold a hand
To light my world
By lighting another's light
For when we shine
We are expelling the darkness
So please, please don't dim my light
For if you do
The others I touch
Will see your darkness
Instead of the light.
Be the light
In a world of darkness! ♥

Giving

I love this—there is power in the giving!
When we give
We step out of our circumstance
We brighten the light in others
Which shines back on us
I challenge you to give it a try
It might change your life
And your circumstance

Shine your light; see the reflection ♥

Kindness Matters

Be kind

Chapter Fifteen | Soul Whispers From Maggie

Kindness matters ♥

The Song

You raise me up

It's important to be people who raise others up!
Be an encourager!
When you see a weakness in others
Help them rise above it
Be authentic in love

This song speaks
Loudly to me
To be an encourager

This world is full of people
Who for reasons we may never know
Will take people to the mountain
Only to knock them down

Be authentic in love
Be encouragers!

Recently in my life
Someone I respected
Seeing weakness in me
Made a choice *not* to raise me up
Used words and actions to crush my spirit

Shining the light on the faults of others

Reflects back on the character of us, my friends
And does not raise either up

Be authentic in love
Be encouragers!

I cast no fault
Because in my past
I too have used my words
To crush and wound
So I remind you again

Be authentic in love
Be encouragers! ♥

My Shamrock

The wisdom of the shamrock
Do you know how many times in the last two years my shamrock plant has appeared dead?
Do you know how many times I have sat it outside, planning to throw it out, only to see life rising back to it!
This morning as I looked at it, Spirit spoke to me. "There is a lesson in that shamrock!"
Just because life loses its spark, value, or leaves, in the roots there is still life. Nourish those wounded, lifeless, broken plants in your life, and you might see the miracle of new growth.
Nourish what you see as death in others and watch them come to life!

Chapter Fifteen | Soul Whispers From Maggie

Be encouragers of greatness to those who have lost hope!
♥

I Choose

I choose
Earlier this year, I spoke in Haileybury, about living an authentic life
I no longer live with the mask of performance
I no longer live with the mask of acceptance
I choose to live without regret
I choose to be a powerful ripple
I choose to give acceptance
I choose love ♥
Love of myself
Love of others
I choose freedom
Freedom for myself
Freedom for others
I choose grace
Grace for myself
Grace for others
Have a powerful, enlightened Wednesday!
Much love ♥

Catching a Ride

Catching a ride
Sometimes in life
You need to catch a ride with someone
Who is stronger than you

Who can fly higher than you!
If you see strength in me, hop on and rest your weary wings
Then when you're ready
Swoop down and pick up someone else you see struggling
To be in the arena of courageous living
We must encourage and lift up one another! ♥

The Human Experience

We are all living the human experience with human emotions—highs, lows, likes, dislikes, good experiences, bad experiences, exhilarating moments, as well as suffocating challenging times and whether we like it or not we all experience wounding life moments because if we did not, we would not be living the human experience!

None of us are exempt, not mothers, fathers, teachers, leaders, pastors, therapists, coaches, and not even death doulas. We all live, learn, and repeatedly evolve—each time gaining new lessons, insights, and strengths.

Even the greatest teachers and leaders have shown us their human experience. Is Oprah always living life as her highest self? Holy shit, no! She is living the human experience with all the flaws and weaknesses that go with that.

The key is to be gentle with each other on this journey, knowing and accepting that we are all human and susceptible to human emotion.

Chapter Fifteen | Soul Whispers From Maggie

We love because we are loved.
We forgive because we are forgiven.
We share because we have experienced lack.
We listen because we have been heard.
We teach because we have been taught.

So when you experience human experiences.

Pause, connect, be mindful ♥

I Am

Sometimes,
In the stillness of the night, we are awakened to be reminded who we are by remembering what we are *not*.
I am *not* my thoughts!
I am *not* my circumstance!
I am *not* my feelings!
But,
I *am* me
I *am* created with purpose
I *am* passionate
I *am* compassionate
I *am* divinely spirituality gifted
I *am* peace, love, light
I *am* powerful
I *am* enough

My friends who are struggling, let what you are *not* remind you of what you *are*!

The *I AM* statements are permanent steadfast truths—let that sink into your soul ♥

Sit With *You*

"When you can't look on the bright side
I will sit with you in your darkness." Jules de Gaultier

This is what Death Doulas specialize in, but remember,
We are not exempt from feeling the darkness of life as well.
This has been a challenging week of darkness coming in on me.
It comes in like a dark cloud hovering just at the edge of reality
From the loss of a dear friend,
A family member's bad health diagnosis,
And some personal challenges myself
Sadness, loss, and grief can hit our lives at any time.
Sometimes we sit in the darkness with others,
And sometimes we need others to hold space for us. ♥

Never give up my friends, we are not alone! ♥

Broken People Wound

You can't fix yourself
By breaking someone else

I'm so sorry to all the people I "broke" before I learned to heal myself!

I send you love and healing to the wounds I may have caused!

I hope that you now see and understand that anger usually comes from a place of deep pain.

So when you encounter an angry person, send them love, because most likely they are deeply wounded!

Be blessed today! ♥

Gratitude Journal – Day 27

Write about someone you love.

I love my children with agape love—the unconditional love that keeps no record of wrong. My love for them *never* waivers (unlike my "like" for them, lol)!

From the first time I felt them move inside me, love was there. The saying, "There is nothing like a mother's love," was simply words until that point. And then I looked into their tiny faces, and love grew deeper than I could ever imagine.

This love—the mother's love—next to the Creator's love, is the strongest bond of love that I have ever felt.

I would give my life for my children based on that love—not based on anything done on their part, and not based on that love being returned.

Simply unconditional love ♥

Gratitude Day 21

Write about something that you do every day and why you're grateful for it.

Every single day I wake up breathing, I am grateful to breathe with ease every single day. I am grateful to be alive, and I am grateful that I understand how precious life is.

Another thing that I do every single day is to have my morning coffee. I am grateful for that delicious hot coffee in the peace and tranquility of my home.

I also get love from my dog, every single day, it is quite ironic that *dog* backward is *God*. Both give love freely and unconditionally. I am grateful that every single day, I can connect with Spirit. Sometimes watching and noticing how interactions happen with such synchronization beyond belief.

I am grateful that I am now at a place in my life where I notice those things. I am thankful for the memories of how far I have come.

I am grateful for personal growth every single day! ♥

Then and Now

What a difference a year makes.
Think back, then and now,
How am I different, and why am I grateful.

Chapter Fifteen | Soul Whispers From Maggie

Wow!

The first thing to come to mind was "job"—last year I had a job, this year I don't. I am grateful that happened, although not so much the way it happened. My job frustrated me, did not inspire me, and their core values did not line up with mine, but they paid me money. Was the money worth all that I was giving up for it? I am grateful for my partner and his ability and willingness to take on most of my financial stress, giving me the break I had never had in my adult life. I am grateful for that.

The authentic me is completely different. I like myself, my choices, my goals, my life. People and things that I never thought I could live without have moved, changed, or left. My children are on their life journeys, and I have found more peace and balance by getting out of their way and not trying to *own* their journey. My love is not based on owning their path. I am grateful for that.

Last year I was committed to healing the broken and wounded pieces of my life. I had to do a lot of releasing, forgiving, and letting go. Those things were replaced with peace, contentment, gratitude, and hope. Those life experiences, as difficult as they were, grew me to a better version of myself.

I am grateful, blessed, and happy with my life.
I have learned in the past year, like never before in my life, that I am never alone, even when alone!

I encourage everyone reading this to take your healing journey of self-discovery. ♥

Happy Birthday in Heaven

Happy Birthday, Momma
The heavens received you
The earth grieved you
Yet you are forever here
At least for me
You are never far
My heart holds you close
As I remember the past
My only regret
To have loved you more
Sing loud today Momma
Dance and celebrate
As I honor your birthday! ♥♥♥

I Love Morning

In the stillness of the morning
I hear
The quiet of the world
The humming of my furnace
The birds outside my window chirping
The gentle music of the wind chimes
I feel
That peaceful beat of my heart
My hands the warmth of my coffee cup
My skin the coolness of the morning chill

Chapter Fifteen | Soul Whispers From Maggie

I smell
As I smell its aroma
I closed my eyes
It awakens my senses
In the distance, the scent of sandalwood
I taste
I treasure the taste of that first sip
That morning coffee
The nectar of the gods
I feel
I feel its warmth as I slowly swallow
It warms my soul, I'm sure
To feel the quiet stillness
This morning
The chirping reminding me
My soul is at peace
In the stillness of the quiet morning
My heart is full of gratitude
I love the quiet mornings
They energize my soul
From deep within my being
I feel it rise within
That power deep within, gently singing
It is well with my soul

I Am *Me*

I am not who I was
I am who I am
I am who I was born to be
I am me, I am
I own it

I step up
I claim my identity
I am authentic, I am
That old me
The one in the mask me
She left
To make room for authentic me
Free me
Authentic me
Happy me
Intuitive me
Worthy me
Peaceful me
Contented me
In love with myself me
Unapologetic me ♥♥♥

Guilt

Self-guilt
Our destructive enemy
Not our friend
Let it go ♥

Hear Me

Spirit speaks
Can you hear?
Quiet your noise
Settle your heart
Quiet your head
Deep in your being

Chapter Fifteen | Soul Whispers From Maggie

Spirit speaks
You know it's me
When ego's gone
Spirit speaks
Can you hear? ♥

Early Morning

I love to wake up early
Whilst most are still asleep
With the angels, I'm up early
In the stillness
I feel their presence
Their caresses to my soul
Oh the beauty of the stillness
Before the dawn
Pure tranquility
In the quiet, she speaks
My higher self
No ego, no shame, no regret
I stretch my arms
I feel her embrace
In silence, we connect
I am brought to tears
The power, the love, the strength, the beauty
The soul
The God of this creation
Embedded the soul
For all that I need
To nourish and to grow
Embedded in the soul
Oh the beauty of the stillness

As I embrace my soul ♥

The Healer

Compassion, emotional security, generosity, self-love, and self-care, healer.
I am comfortable in my skin. I love, cherish, and nurture myself.

I am the best friend to myself. My relationships with others reflect my security in knowing I am worthy of love and respect.

I heal myself, so I can be the change I want to see in the world, and so my compassion can inspire others.

I am healed I am; my spirit says fly, my child, fly! ♥

In love and light,
Maggie

About The Author

Maggie Morris

Maggie is an Authentic Caring, Sensitive Soul with a Passion for nurturing others with her Soul love. Maggie lives her gifts of service to humanity through her generosity and her ability to ignite the flame in others to see their limitless possibilities. Maggie uses her intuition and connection with Spirit to be an example of strength and courage to all she meets. As a Life Coach, Mindfulness Mentor, Meditation Facilitator, and Death Doula, Maggie continues to pursue her passions as well as help those she connects with to find Healing. You can reach Maggie through her website at www.whispersofwisdom.ca.

www.ingramcontent.com/pod-product-compliance
Lightning Source LLC
Chambersburg PA
CBHW062008070426
42451CB00008BA/275